Eating right means eating
healthy food.

It is okay to eat some treats,
but only a little. Fruits and
vegetables are better for you
than cookies and candy.

Eat fruits and vegetables every day. Bread, rice, nuts, and milk are good, too.

Your body needs healthy food to be strong. It needs healthy food to feel good.

Put good food on one plate to make a healthy meal. You will be glad you did. This food looks very good, doesn't it? Yum, yum!

Always eat the right food at school. Eat the food that is good for you.

"I am proud of you," your mom will say. You will be proud, too. You will feel good!

Good manners are also part of eating right. Here are some things you should do when you eat.

1. Wash your hands before you eat.

2. Use a napkin to wipe your hands and mouth.

3. Do not throw food. It is very messy!

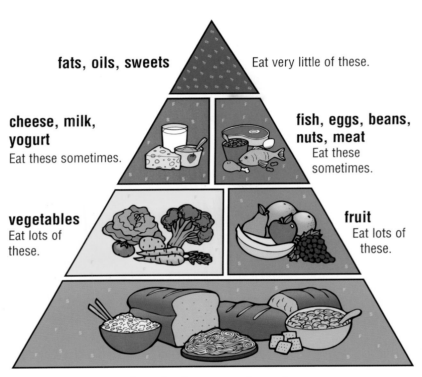

fats, oils, sweets Eat very little of these.

cheese, milk, yogurt
Eat these sometimes.

fish, eggs, beans, nuts, meat
Eat these sometimes.

vegetables
Eat lots of these.

fruit
Eat lots of these.

bread, rice, cereal, pasta
Eat lots of these, too.

Eat healthy food each day. The food pyramid shows you what to eat.